Women, Baptists
and
Ordination

Celebrating ...
    Affirming ...
        Encouraging ...
the Ordained Ministry of Women
in Baptist Churches

Baptist Union
of Great Britain
www.baptist.org.uk

Published on behalf of The Baptist Union of Great Britain
by Nigel Lynn Publishing and Marketing Ltd
106 High Street, Milton under Wychwood, Chipping Norton
Oxfordshire, OX7 6ET, United Kingdom
enquiries@nigellynnpublishing.com

The Baptist Union of Great Britain
Baptist House, 129 Broadway, Didcot
Oxfordshire, OX11 8RT, United Kingdom

This book was compiled by Tricia Troughton, assisted by members of the Baptist Union's staff

The Scripture quotations contained herein are from the New Revised Standard Version of the
Bible, Anglicized Edition, copyright © 1989, 1995 by the Division of Christian Education of
the National Council of the Churches of Christ in the United States of America, and are used
by permission. All rights reserved

British Library Cataloguing in Publication Data
Data available

ISBN-10   0 901472 44 1
ISBN-13   978 0 901472 44 1

1 3 5 7 9 10 8 6 4 2

Printed in the United Kingdom
on acid-free paper by
The Alden Group, Oxford

Contents

Foreword

For over eighty years the Baptist Union of Great Britain has encouraged the ordination of women and affirmed their contribution to the life and mission of Baptist churches. Whilst I believe this is a cause for celebration, there remains a concern that this recognition has not always been outworked in the context of the local church.

This booklet has two basic purposes. Firstly, it addresses the question of whether there are any grounds on which we can deny the ordained ministry to women. Secondly, it is an invitation for Baptists to take a fresh look at the Scriptures concerning the ministry of ordained women.

I am well aware that our Declaration of Principle states that each church has liberty, under the guidance of the Holy Spirit, to interpret and administer the laws of Christ. But equally I am reminded of the Christians in Berea who examined the Bible on a daily basis to test whether what they were being told was in line with the teaching of the Scriptures (Acts 17.11).

I encourage ministers, leaders and church members to bring an openness of mind and heart to a debate which can so often cause pain and distress in the local church. We need to make space to explore the question of biblical equality and whether the ordained ministry should be denied anyone on the grounds of their gender. If we discover there is a golden thread of biblical equality running through the Scriptures, then we must pose the question, how can we place any limits on the ministry gifts and abilities of Christian women?

Although this is a booklet on the ministry of ordained women, I believe that as we study the subject we will discover the mission potential for the local church. In a world where women are often excluded by the church, I believe that any church which practises biblical equality is demonstrating that the Gospel of Jesus Christ is in every sense *Good News* for men and women.

David Coffey
General Secretary

Aims

The aims of this booklet are

1. to help Baptist churches to consider the basis on which women as well as men exercise their varied gifts and ministries, by looking at Scripture afresh and revisiting the journey so far

2. to encourage Baptist churches in affirming, recognising and developing the ordained ministries of women in their midst

3. to encourage Baptist women who sense a call to ministry, are in training or who are already ordained

4. to encourage Baptist churches to be open to the variety of people whom God is calling to serve amongst them in ordained ministry

… in Christ Jesus you are all children of God through faith. As many of you as were baptized into Christ have clothed yourselves with Christ. There is no longer Jew or Greek, there is no longer slave or free, there is no longer male and female; for all of you are one in Christ Jesus.

Galatians 3.26–8

We will look at

- some theology
- some testimonies
- some questions
- and some further resources

Many people find change hard

Tradition can be a strong basis for building sound family and community patterns, but sometimes it stifles life-giving change and can tie communities to outmoded practices. Sometimes damaging prejudices are preserved without question with detrimental results for whole groups and individuals. Occasionally even the Scriptures are used unhelpfully to preserve the status quo rather than to allow God's will to be revealed by the Spirit.

Sometimes the gifts of women are stifled by the traditions of the church, by attitudes of individuals or churches and by unhelpful structures and practices. When this happens it is necessary to restate the basis on which previous decisions have been made in order to highlight the experience and blessings of individuals' lives and to enable groups of people to make a journey that leads them further into the exciting diversity and fullness of life that God intends.

Which Bible?

Reading the Scriptures today

Unless otherwise stated, we have used the New Revised Standard Version (NRSV) of the Scriptures, because it makes a distinction between words that mean 'humankind' and include male and female in their meaning where that was the sense of the original text. Previous translations, though sometimes favoured because of familiarity or beauty of language, can change the meaning of particular passages that are especially relevant to this booklet.

We need to be aware that language and its translation can alter the meaning of the original, and can sometimes obscure the presence of women – for example:

Romans 12.1

> *I beseech you therefore, brethren …*   AV/KJV
>
> *Therefore I urge you, brothers …*   NIV
>
> *I appeal to you therefore, brothers and sisters …*   NRSV

Romans 12.6

> *Having then gifts differing according to the grace that is given to us, whether prophecy, let us prophesy according to the proportion of faith.*   AV/KJV
>
> *We have different gifts, according to the grace given us. If a man's gift is prophesying, let him use it in prophesying to his faith.*   NIV
>
> *We have gifts that differ according to the grace given to us: prophecy, in proportion to faith.*   NRSV

There is a need to look more deeply to understand whether language is reflecting what was meant in the original text.

In the past, English words such as 'brethren', 'man' and 'his' were commonly used to mean both women and men.

More recent translations clarify this by using inclusive language when scholars believe the original text meant women as well as men.

The Journey So Far

It is God's story

So God created humankind in his image,
in the image of God he created them;
male and female he created them.

Genesis 1.27

In the beginning was the Word,
and the Word was with God,
and the Word was God.
He was in the world and the world came into being through him:
yet the world did not know him.
He came to what was his own, and his own people did not accept him.
But to all who received him, who believed in his name, he gave power to become children of God, who were born, not of blood or of the will of the flesh, or of the will of man, but of God.

John 1.1,10–13

Since the earliest days of the church, both women and men have given themselves to Christ and used the gifts that he has given them in varied and often sacrificial ways to advance the gospel of Christ and to build up his body, the church.

The gifts he gave were that some would be apostles, some prophets, some evangelists, some pastors and teachers, to equip the saints for the work of ministry, for building up the body of Christ, until all of us come to the unity of the faith and of the knowledge of the Son of God, to maturity, to the measure of the full stature of Christ.

Ephesians 4.11–13

Church history

We will be looking at women in the Scriptures later in this booklet, but it is also important to look at those who were prominent in church history.

Numerous Christian women from the past were, and still are, valued for their insight and wisdom. Many of them were leading thinkers who predated the first Baptist churches and the Reformation.

- Hilda of Whitby
- Julian of Norwich
- Hildegard of Bingen
- Teresa of Avila

Others had an undisputed role in missionary activity and social reform.

- Gladys Aylward in China
- Mary Slessor in Nigeria
- Florence Nightingale: the establishment of nursing
- Mary Secole: a prominent nurse in the Crimean War
- Elizabeth Fox: reform in prisons

Yet others wrote hymns that helped to explain and maintain Christian doctrine in an age before education was widely available.

- Fanny Crosby: 'To God be the Glory', 'Blessed Assurance' and many more
- Mrs Alexander: 'All things bright and beautiful', 'There is a green hill far away'
- Frances Ridley Havergal: 'Take my life and let it be'
- Charlotte Elliott: 'Just as I am'

Baptist beginnings

Baptist churches have existed in Britain since the early seventeenth century. In those early days women preached, taught, founded churches, took part in discussion in church meetings, and were freely encouraged to do so. Baptist churches were proud of their radical stance and taught the involvement of all according to the gifts given by God. The Revd Dr Ruth Gouldbourne has written a detailed history of women and ministry in English Baptist church life (see *Further Reading*, page 33).

Baptists in the eighteenth and nineteenth centuries

As Baptists became more numerous, influential and 'respectable' during the eighteenth and nineteenth centuries, the organisation of church life took on a more institutional and conformist shape, and 'ordination to ministry' was introduced. This was a way of recognising and accrediting the gifts of individuals called to pastor and to teach in individual churches.

Churches of other denominations, and society in general, were able to understand this arrangement. But sometimes the 'ordained ministry' is thought of as indicating a hierarchical arrangement within the church with 'the minister' carrying authority in a way that is contrary to a Baptist understanding of the gathered community of Christians. Baptists believe that any leadership structure in a church is under the authority of the Spirit of God as discerned through the contribution of every member as they assemble together in the church meeting.

During these centuries the role of women in Baptist churches became more restricted. The pattern of life in society became more organised as employment was increasingly linked with growing industrialisation. Women had fewer opportunities for education than men, and were far less likely to work outside the home – except in menial tasks and in factories. The opportunity for women to contribute God-given gifts and insights was quite restricted.

Baptist 'ministry' became more and more identified as meaning 'ordained pastors', and women began to be barred from joining in discussion and from voting in church meetings.

Baptists in the twentieth century

In the early twentieth century, the Baptist Union took over the running of the Deaconesses order (established in 1890), and opened the first training college for women offering theological and practical training.

During the 1920s and 1930s Deaconesses were often called to pastor new mission churches, or to work in weaker established churches. By the late 1940s they were often in full charge of old and new fellowships in very difficult circumstances. They did the same work as male 'ministers', but with little recognition and with less pay.

Alongside these developments, the Baptist Union was challenged to recognise that a female 'minister', Edith Gates, had been called to the churches of Little Tew and Clevely in 1918. In 1922 she was added to the official list of probationer ministers.

In 1925 the Baptist Union Council officially accepted the call of women to pastorates after lengthy deliberations of a committee set up to examine the issues involved.

The twenty-first century

In the eighty years since the first Baptist woman was ordained as a minister, there have been enormous changes in society and in the church. Girls now have access to equal opportunities in education and achieve higher grades than boys at GCSE, AS and A level. More women than men go on to study at university. Women are found in almost every area of employment using God-given talents and abilities to the full after many struggles caused by past traditions, 'old boys' networks and prejudiced attitudes. Where women have found their way into the law, medicine, science, engineering and many other previously male-dominated areas of employment, their contribution is undeniable. A diverse work-force can yield rich gains. Patterns of work become more life-giving, and men as well as women are freer to contribute to home and family life.

Changes in church life inevitably reflect changes in society and the church has to guard against retaining old-fashioned patterns and practices for which there are no bases in doctrine or belief. There is a need to pray, discuss and study Scripture in order to determine God's will for the present time.

Where Christians in this country have openly discussed the issues involved, the result has generally been a much wider acceptance of women in ordained ministry. In many instances women and men are now found using gifts for ministry to make disciples, to teach and to preach in obedience to the call of God.

Today there are well over a hundred ordained Baptist women exercising ministries in churches, hospitals, schools, colleges, prisons and the armed forces. God undoubtedly calls, equips and blesses the ministry of women as well as men.

We will meet some of them later in this booklet, but now let us turn to the Scriptures.

The Scriptures in Question

If we look at a broad sweep of Scripture we can trace God's intention through the ages.

The Old Testament

A number of women play a prominent role in the life of the people of God.

- Esther – a whole book about her
- Ruth – a whole book about her
- Rahab – found in Joshua 2
- Deborah – found in Judges 4 and 5

God constantly surprises us by not working in the way that society expects.

God spoke through the prophet Joel

I will pour out my Spirit on all flesh; your sons and daughters shall prophesy, your old men shall dream dreams, and your young men shall see visions. Even on the male and female slaves, in those days, I will pour out my spirit.

Joel 2.28, 29

This prophecy, fulfilled at Pentecost and quoted by Peter (Acts 2.17,18) makes a point of including both women and men as receivers of God's Spirit.

Jesus' life story ...

- ... clearly shows an attitude towards women that challenged the ideas of the people of the day.
- Mary, his mother, was chosen by God and gave herself totally. She had great insight into God's way of working (Luke 1.46–55).
- Anna the prophetess received the baby in the temple (Luke 2.36–8).
- Jesus' conversation with the woman at the well broke the conventions of the time (John 4).

WOMEN, BAPTISTS AND ORDINATION

- Jesus taught Mary and Martha. That was more important to him than Martha's preparation of a meal (Luke 10.38–42). Later Martha showed similar faith and insight to Peter (*see* Matthew 16.16) when she said 'Yes, Lord, I believe you are the Messiah, the Son of God, the one coming into the world' (John 11.27).

- Jesus affirmed the prophetic action and understanding of a woman as she anointed his feet.

  By pouring this ointment on my body she has prepared me for burial. Truly I tell you, wherever this good news is proclaimed in the whole world, what she has done will be told in remembrance of her.

  Matthew 26.6–13

- Jesus appeared to Mary and also to a group of women after the resurrection and commissioned them to tell the disciples that he was alive (John 20.10–18 and Luke 24).

The Early Church

The Scriptures do not give us a 'blue-print' of how the church should organise itself, and so through the centuries we find variations across and within the denominations. They do, however, suggest that there are some fundamental principles involved in church life.

Principles

The New Creation

So if anyone is in Christ, there is a new creation: everything old has passed away; see, everything has become new!

2 Corinthians 5.17

As many of you as were baptized into Christ have clothed yourselves with Christ. There is no longer Jew or Greek, there is no longer slave or free, there is no longer male and female' for all of you are one in Christ Jesus.

Galatians 3.27–28

Love

I give you a new commandment, that you love one another. Just as I have loved you, you also should love one another. By this everyone will know that you are my disciples, if you have love for one another.

John 13.34, 35

Humility, patience, peace and unity

I therefore, the prisoner in the Lord, beg you to lead a life worthy of the calling to which you have been called, with all humility and gentleness, with patience, bearing with one another in love, making every effort to maintain the unity of the Spirit in the bond of peace.

Ephesians 4.1–3
see also Philippians 2.1–11

Maturity

Gifts are given so that the church grows to maturity in Christ – *see* Ephesians 4.11–13.

Servanthood

To be truly great means to serve all – *see* Matthew 20.26–8.

Transformation

I appeal to you therefore, brothers and sisters, by the mercies of God, to present your bodies as a living sacrifice, holy and acceptable to God, which is your spiritual worship. Do not be conformed to this world, but be transformed by the renewing of your minds, so that you may discern what is the will of God – what is good, acceptable and perfect.

Romans 12.1–2

Respect

… in humility regard others as better than yourselves.

Philippians 2.3

Mutual Submission

Be subject to one another out of reverence for Christ.

Ephesians 5.21

Practice

Scripture gives some insights into how these principles were worked out in practice, but very little detail about the actual organisation of the early church. Deacons and elders/bishops are mentioned with the emphasis on personal qualities and mature faith. It is clear that everyone worked together for the gospel with each one playing their part in the body according to their gifts. Christ is the head of the body, the church.

see 1 Corinthians 12 and Romans 12

People

Romans 16.1–16 contains the longest list of names in any New Testament letter. Paul mentions twenty-six Christians, twenty-four of them by name. Over a third of those mentioned are women, which is unusual given the male-dominated society of the time. The warmth and kindness in his greetings emphasises the importance of friendship in the work. The inclusion of the names of nine gifted women in the list is strong evidence against the theory that Paul had a low view of women's ministry.

• *Phoebe* was a gentile Christian named after a Greek goddess. She was probably a wealthy woman on a business trip to Rome. She may have been the bearer of the letter to the Romans, and Paul commends her to the community in Rome, rather as we would write a reference for someone. She served as a deacon in her church fellowship in Cenchrea, the seaport for the city of Corinth.

• *Priscilla* is mentioned in a number of places in the New Testament (Acts 18.2, 18.26–8; 1 Corinthians 16.19; 2 Timothy 4.19) usually before her husband Aquila. This may indicate that she was converted first, or that she had a more prominent ministry in the church, or that she was a titled lady. She and Aquila opened their home and together served as spiritual mentors to young missionaries.

- *Junia*, the wife of Andronicus. Both are described as 'outstanding among the apostles'.

- *Mary*, *Tryphena* and *Tryphosa* (meaning Delicate and Dainty!), and *Persis* – four women are the only Christians commended by Paul for their hard work in the Lord's name.

- *Rufus' mother* – described as 'mother' to the apostle too.

- *Julia* and the unnamed sister of Nereus are also mentioned in this list.

- *Priscilla* and *Aquila* travelled with Paul when he went on to Syria, but were left in Ephesus where it seems they established the church together.

- In Acts 21 Luke writes of the four daughters of the evangelist Philip who had the gift of prophesy.

- *Euodias* and *Synthyche* are mentioned in Philippians 4.2–3 by name.

- *Mary, Lydia, Prisca, Phoebe, Nympha* and *Apphia* were all amongst 'patronesses' who opened their homes to new churches.

Problem passages

There are, however, some so-called 'problem passages' whose interpretation is difficult and disputed, and which are sometimes quoted where the ministry of women is not fully accepted. Here are some examples.

> **Women cannot be ministers because Paul said 'I permit no woman to teach or to have authority over a man; she is to keep silent' (1 Timothy 2.11–15).**

17

- Scripture needs to be read in the context of whole passages and of the culture of the day, and alongside other passages.

- In Paul's day, women were not expected to learn in the synagogue. Paul may have been suggesting that women should not talk to each other during teaching, but should learn alongside the men.

- Women definitely did speak in church in his time. Paul also said 'any woman who prays or prophesies with her head uncovered disgraces her head' (1 Corinthians 11.5). The culture of the day demanded that women cover their heads when praying or prophesying because not to do so could mean a woman was of ill-repute. We no longer adhere to these particular words of Paul, and need to look at other verses with the same culturally aware discernment.

- In Paul's day women were regarded as socially inferior to men. The freedom of women found in the early church is all the more surprising. It indicates the changing order brought about by the death and resurrection of Christ. Submission to one another rather than domination by one gender over another is suggested as the new Christian standard in relationships (Ephesians 5.21).

- Paul taught the church to value every part of the body equally. When teaching about the emerging order in the early church he also adds 'Nevertheless in the Lord woman is not independent of man, nor is man independent of woman. For just as woman came from man, so man comes from woman; but all things come from God' (1 Corinthians 11.12).

  Leadership is male. The order is Christ, Men, Women.
  see Ephesians 5.22–33

- This passage follows on from v.21 'submit to one another out of reverence to Christ'. Submission to one another is the basis for relationships in the church as a whole. Paul then describes the basis of the marriage relationship for Christians. Submission and love replace domination and ownership as required Christian qualities. These new attitudes developed in response to the transforming work of Christ through the Holy Spirit.

• Within the church, Christ is the head. Christians form the body in which each member has equal status.

• Examples of women who were leaders in the early church have already been given.

• Our understanding of 'leadership' needs to be transformed. Christ taught and modelled leadership that is based on servanthood. He contrasted that pattern with the exercising of authority based on status alone.

The kings of the Gentiles lord it over them; and those in authority over them are called benefactors. But not so with you; rather the greatest among you must become like the youngest, and the leader like one who serves.

see Luke 22.24–7

Conclusions from Scripture

It is clear from this broad look at Scripture, despite the so-called 'problem passages', that God's redemptive work involves both women and men in ways that are often surprising.

New converts to the faith formed churches where both women and men were clearly using their resources to the full despite the culture of the day.

The Story Continued

The present day

In the present day, the wider Baptist family is being blessed and built up by the ordained ministry of many women, some of whom are listed below.

* Myra Blyth – former Deputy General Secretary of the Baptist Union, and now tutor at Regent's Park College

* Ruth Bottoms – Moderator of the Baptist Union Trustee Board

* Kate Coleman – minister of The Regeneration Centre, Birmingham and President of the Baptist Union 2006–7

* Mary Cotes – ecumenical Moderator of Milton Keynes

* Ruth Gouldbourne – minister of Bloomsbury Central Baptist Church, London

* Lynn Green – minister of Wokingham Baptist Church and chair of the appointments committee of the Baptist Union

* Viv O'Brien – Ministries Adviser of the Baptist Union of Great Britain

* Pat Took – Regional Minister and Team Leader for the Metropolitan region of the Baptist Union

* Anne Wilkinson-Hayes – Regional Minister for the Baptist Union of Victoria, Australia

* Sheila Martin, Kathryn Morgan and Helen Wordsworth – Regional Ministers

There are many others, often less well-known, who work in every area of the country as pastors and in a variety of other situations where ordained ministry is required.

On the following six pages are some examples of women who have been called, recognised, trained and accredited to exercise Christian ministry as Baptists.

My name is **Catriona Gorton**. I have been a minister at Hugglescote Baptist Church for the past two years. I am helping my small, mostly older, congregation to develop new ways of being church and doing mission following the closure of our building – developing community links and encouraging contemporary approaches to worship. I have overseen setting up a teens group and a 'mobile lunch club'. I also chair Churches Together and coordinate the ecumenical holiday club. Exhausting and rewarding!

My name is the Revd **Joy Owen**. I have been in pastoral ministry in South Wales for nine years, for the last five years at Moriah Baptist Church, Abercynon.

When God calls he equips! The pastoral and preaching and teaching gifts he has given me have been used to bring others to Christ, and to encourage them to use their giftings also. As a body of Christians in this place we are on a steep learning curve, keeping in step with the Holy Spirit. Those of us called to minister as leaders don't wake up one morning and think 'I fancy being a minister'. It's hard, a continual moving from the comfort zone! But when we see God moving powerfully in the lives of those to whom we minister, then glimpses of the kingdom are possible.

My name is **Patricia Took** and I have been in ministry for twenty-one years. I was called to the ministry after my third child was born and served for thirteen years at Leytonstone in East London. I was then called to be Metropolitan Superintendent, becoming Team Leader of the LBA when re-structuring took place. The sense of God's call, first to the ministry and later to the London role, was inescapable. I have loved every minute of it.

My name is **Barbara Carpenter**. I have been a minister at Bradninch Baptist Church for the past four months, having been here as the student minister for the previous three years. I'm also currently serving as the Baptist chaplain at the University of Exeter. The road to ordained ministry wasn't an easy one – I'd worked particularly in the areas of retreats and spiritual direction, not typical Baptist stuff, for a number of years – but thanks to the encouragement and support of a number of people (many of them women!) I find myself ministering here in Devon as God's person – and loving it!

I (**Judith Wheatley**) am involved in ministry with children, young people and their families at Anderson Baptist Church in Reading. I have worked within Scouting to make links into the community. We have acheived this with great success and are now looking at ways to stregthen links between the youthwork and the church. We are also involved in an exciting schools work project which resources the twelve local primary schools and two secondary schools, aiming to work in partnership to deliver high quality religious education in our area.

My name is **Jill Willett**. I have been the Baptist minister at Greenhill Community Church – a Baptist/Anglican Local Ecumenical Partnership since 2001, when the Partnership started – the first two years as Student Pastor. We are a growing church on a council estate on the edges of Coalville in Leicestershire. Since 2001, the congregation has doubled in size, the membership growing from thirty-two to sixty-eight. Since September 2004, we have had twelve baptisms, and have seen God really working with the young people. God is amazing!

The picture above shows my husband Martyn and myself baptising one of our young people, Wesley Edge. Wes had just won a gold medal at the Special Olympics in Glasgow, for tennis. He became a Christian in May last year at a 24/7 prayer event.

My name is **Rosemary Kidd**. I worked for six years with Newall Green Baptist Church, Wythenshawe, net-working with other Baptist ministers of small churches on disadvantaged housing estates. This picture shows us constructing a 'dreamweaver' during an all-age worship service, symbolising our

visions and dreams for future mission, as filtered through the bright golden threads of the cross. I have always worked ecumenically and I am totally committed to *Unity in Diversity*. I currently combine non-stipendiary Baptist ministry in a Baptist, Methodist and URC Local Ecumenical Partnership on the edge of the Derbyshire Peak District with a full-time training and development role in the Methodist Connexion. I resource churches in all sorts of ways: for example, good practice for pastoral visitors; child protection policy and practice; ideas for children's ministry and youth workers; all-age worship for preachers; working with adults; Powerpoint® from scratch; and conflict transformation for ministers.

My name is **Kathryn Bracewell**, and I've been the minister of Thomas Helwys Baptist Church in Nottingham for over eight years now. I often say to people 'When you stumble across the best Baptist church in England, then you're in no hurry to leave it!' I find ministry to be deeply challenging and enormously interesting, and I love seeing people respond to God and find purpose and hope for their lives.

My name is **Diane Holmes** and I've been an associate minister at Ashby Baptist Church for the past two and a half years. My special responsibility is for older people and in developing that work I have needed to be creative as well as pastoral, angry as well as funny, lonely as well as blessed … as drawing alongside older people is to draw alongside the more isolated and often marginalised members of our community – and as far as I know, there are very few, if any, older people's specialists.

My name is **Edith Dawson** and I have been a minister at Kirton in Lindsey for six and a half years, and I'm now at Moss Side in Manchester. I am also chaplain to Humberside and South Yorkshire Army Cadet Force.

My journey to ministry was not without a struggle and I experienced the pain of the Scottish Baptist Union rejection of women's ministry in 1997. The subsequent vote in 1999 allowed SBU churches the 'right' to call the 'person' whom they believed was God's person; however, there is still very little movement in affirming that viewpoint.

I am a politically motivated person caring especially for those who struggle to get their voice heard. I have discovered that 'rural' and 'inner city' ministries have similar challenges in accessing services, with great pockets of isolation and deprivation. I am committed to working out what it means to be a disciple where we are, knowing that as a minister I have the chance to opt out and move on to another 'challenge'.

My name is **Sheila Martin**. I have been one of the Regional Ministers in the Eastern Baptist Association since December 2005. Before that I ministered at Erdington (Six Ways) in Birmingham and at Landbeach and Milton in Cambridge. One of my driving ambitions is to see healthy churches making Jesus known to those around them. The photo is of the induction of a new minister at one of our Essex Baptist Churches.

I am the Revd **Lynn Britten**, minister of Little Lane Church LEP in Bradford. I have been minister of Little Lane since November 2003. The church is a partnership of Baptist, Methodist and United Reformed Christians. It is situated in a predominantly Muslim area with communities of Filipino, Caribbean and European workers. I trained initially at Northumbria Bible College, then worked in a church for two years before training for ordination at Northern Baptist College. Bible college taught me I was a good 'all-rounder'. My main gifts are pastoral care, worship and preaching.

Alvene Kinsey, Church Secretary, writes:

In an LEP of three denominations Lynn is very much appreciated by all, especially for her pastoral care and services. She has had a very positive impact on Little Lane.

The photograph attached is of a Dedication Service. Used with permission.

The Accreditation of Baptist Ministers

Anyone sensing a call to Baptist ministry must first have that call tested and confirmed by their local church and the Association's Ministerial Recognition Committee.

At this point, they will be advised of the next step in the process, which would normally be to undertake ministerial training and formation at one of our five Baptist theological colleges.

On satisfactory completion of training, and upon receiving a call to a qualifying office, a minister would become newly accredited and, after meeting the requirements of the probationary period, would become fully accredited. However, learning does not stop at this point as all ministers are encouraged to continue to engage in lifelong learning and continuing professional development.

Where Do We Go From Here?

Although Baptists have been recognising, training and accrediting women as ministers for over eighty years, there are still some churches and individuals that discourage women who sense a call. There are others that are reluctant to accept women who have already been trained and accredited as Baptist ministers.

Some answers to questions and statements that are sometimes voiced

God is our Father – we need a man at the helm

Genesis says – 'So God created humankind in his own image, in the image of God he created them; male and female he created them' Genesis 1.27.

The image of God is seen most clearly in the complementary natures of female as well as male.

Scripture gives us some images of God that many would acknowledge are more female than male.

An 'every member' approach to ministry is the New Testament norm.

Women were created after men and are inferior to them

The creation narrative is not ordered by rank. If it were we would have to concede that human beings were created after the animals, but God did not intend human beings to be subordinate to them. Human beings were made in the image of God – male and female.

Women were created as man's 'helper' and therefore cannot lead men

The same word for 'helper' is used of God many times in Scripture but that does not prevent God from leading us. Jesus practised and taught servant leadership rather than worldly authoritarian leadership where one 'lords it' over another (*see* Luke 22.24–7).

Jesus only called male disciples – ministers must be male

Living within the social conventions of the time, Jesus could not have called women as his closest disciples. He did however include women amongst his companions. He taught them and entrusted the news of the resurrection to a group of women.

The minister needs his wife to help him run the home/care for the children – how can a woman in ministry cope without a 'wife'?

Patterns in society have changed, particularly in the last thirty years. Many women now work in demanding roles sharing responsibilities for home and family life in a way that is beneficial and life-giving. Patterns of ministry can also change to encourage a fuller use of the gifts of all and a climate of maturity and interdependence in the church as a whole.

The church is full of women. Men do not come to faith and this will be made worse by having a woman minister

It is true that there are more women than men in the church, but this is in a context where the majority of ministers are male!

A woman isn't strong enough emotionally/intellectually to cope with the demands of ministry

The demands of ministry in its traditional form are very great, and many men suffer emotional, mental and physical health problems, or fail in ministry for other reasons. Women tend to be more aware of their emotional strengths and weaknesses and may be more likely to seek the support they need. Women may be better at building a team approach to the work. Intellectually, women are just as able as men.

Some advice when things are difficult

We have never had a woman minister in our church. If we call one, some members say they will leave

Teaching and careful pastoral care are needed in a fellowship where one or two people can influence the church's future in this way. Often attitudes are held in good faith even if they stem from misinterpretation, ignorance or prejudice.

In all areas of contention in church life a programme of teaching and discussion needs to be undertaken with a sensitive understanding of attitudes that are often deeply held. It is important that churches include this subject in their teaching programme, preferably before entering a period of pastoral vacancy.

It is also important that individual members allow God to speak through the weight of opinion in the church meeting after careful and prayerful study and discussion, and do not seek to prevent change through the threat of resignation.

There are plenty of examples of thriving and fruitful churches where ordained women have ministered, or are ministering.

I feel called to ministry but I am not being encouraged to pursue this because I am a woman

Talk to your Regional Minister, or to the Baptist Union Ministry Department. They will arrange a process whereby your call can be tested.

I am experiencing prejudice or discrimination. What can I do?

Contact your regional minister or the Baptist Union ministry department.

I am a minister/minister's spouse/elder/deacon and feel challenged by this teaching – where can I go to discuss how I feel?

Your Regional Minister should be able to suggest suitable people in your area with whom you could talk if you cannot discuss this within your own church.

For further help contact:

- The Baptist Union Department of Ministry
- A Regional Minister
- The ministerial counselling service
- A mentor/spiritual director

Final Conclusions

It is the responsibility of all Christian believers to discover and develop to the full the talents and gifts God gives us, so that we might all mature into Christ-like individuals.

There is no indication from the aforementioned Scriptures that any group of people is excluded from exercising ministry by reason of racial origin, status or gender.

History shows that both women and men have played a vital part in the church from its beginnings.

Our use of spiritual gifts is worked out in every area of our lives – at home; amongst our family, friends and neighbours; in our local community; at work and at leisure.

Specific gifts are used as we contribute to the church, for example through preaching, teaching, pastoral care and administration. Both women and men are sometimes called by God through Baptist churches to give themselves more fully to particular roles in Christian ministry for which ordination is required.